A POCKET GUIDE TO . . .

Satan & the Serpent

A biblical view of Satan and evil

1:1

Answers
IN GENESIS™

Petersburg, Kentucky, USA

Reprinted January 2017

ISBN: 978-1-60092-998-4

Printed in China.

AnswersInGenesis.org

Table of Contents

Introduction

Satan and the origin of evil are hot topics in today's culture. The reality of Satan and the existence of evil are but two areas the world attacks. And the church has few biblical resources on the subject to counter such claims. Some excellent books on this subject include:

> *The Strategy of Satan* by Warren Wiersbe
> *Striving against Satan* by Joel Beeke
> *The Fall of Satan* by Bodie Hodge[1]

This general Pocket Guide is a helpful resource that looks closely at the bad news in Genesis but also shares the powerful good news of Jesus Christ and His sacrifice that has conquered sin, Satan, and evil once for all.

Each question answered is a genuine question that has been asked many times over. These and similar questions are valid questions to ask. To answer them, we need to carefully consider what the Bible says, since it is the only completely reliable source of information about Satan. Although, the Bible doesn't give much information about Satan, angels and other topics since it was written to man[2], it does give enough to reasonably answer most of these questions.

God's Word is infallible and the absolute authority. We need to be leery of absolute conclusions drawn from sources outside the Bible, such as man's ideas or traditions.[3]

---

1. Portions of this pocket guide were taken directly from *The Fall of Satan* by permission of Bodie Hodge.

2. The term "man" in this context refers to mankind as a whole which is commonly and simply called "man" in the Bible but refers to both men and women. Throughout this book, the term "man" is often used for the human race in general. It is not meant in any derogatory or chauvinistic sense, though sometimes it simply means Adam, the first man.

3. Bear in mind that these questions are answered to the best of our ability while using the Bible as the absolute authority. If there is a discrepancy between the Bible and what we have written, then rest assured that we are in error, not the holy Scriptures.

Who Is Satan, and Was He Always Called "Satan"?

by Bodie Hodge

The first use of the name *Satan* is found in 1 Chronicles 21:1; chronologically, this is surpassed by Job which was written much earlier. *Satan* is found throughout Job chapters 1 and 2. Satan (*satan*) literally means *adversary* in Hebrew. The etymology of the name is discussed briefly by Justin Martyr, an early church father, around AD 156. He says,

> Or He meant the devil by the lion roaring against Him: whom Moses calls the serpent, but in Job and Zechariah he is called the devil, and by Jesus is addressed as Satan, showing that a compounded name was acquired by him from the deeds which he performed. For "Sata" in the Jewish and Syrian tongue means apostate; and "Nas" is the word from which he is called by interpretation the *serpent*, i.e., according to the interpretation of the Hebrew term, from both of which there arises the single word Satanas.[1]

Another name appears in the Old Testament in the King James Version:

> How art thou fallen from heaven, O Lucifer, son of the morning! How art thou cut down to the ground, which didst weaken the nations! (Isaiah 14:12 KJV).

This is the only passage that uses the name *Lucifer* to refer to Satan. This name doesn't come from Hebrew but Latin. Perhaps this translation into English was influenced by the *Latin Vulgate*, which uses this name. In Latin, Lucifer means *light-bringer*.

The Hebrew is *heylel* and means *light-bearer, shining one*, or *morning star*. Many modern translations translate this as *star of the morning* or *morning star*. In this passage, *heylel* refers to the king of Babylon and Satan figuratively. Of course, Jesus lays claim to this title in Revelation 22:16. Though the passage in Revelation is in Greek while the passage in Isaiah is Hebrew, both are translated similarly.

Some believe that *Lucifer* was a heavenly or angelic name that was taken from Satan when he rebelled. The Bible doesn't explicitly state this, though Satan is nowhere else referred to as Lucifer but instead is called other names like the *devil, Satan*, etc. This tradition may hold some truth, although the idea seems to miss that this verse is referring to him *during* and *after* his fall—not before. Since other scriptural passages refer to him as Satan, *Lucifer* wasn't necessarily his pre-Fall name any more than *Satan* would be.

Even though Satan is first mentioned by name in Job, previous historical accounts record his actions (see Genesis 3 when Satan influenced the serpent in Revelation 12:9 and Genesis 4 where Cain belonged to him when he slew his brother [1 John 3:12]).

In the New Testament, other names reveal more about Satan's current nature. *Devil* (*diabolos*) means *false accuser, Satan*, and *slanderer* in Greek and is the word from which the English word *diabolical* is formed. Satan is called *dragon* in Revelation 12:9 and Revelation 20:2, as well as the *evil one* in several places. Other names for Satan include *ancient serpent / serpent of old* (Revelation 12:9), *Abaddon* (destruction), *Apollyon* (Destroyer) (Revelation 9:11), *Beelzebub / Beelzebul* (Matthew 12:27), *Belial* (2 Corinthians 6:15), and *tempter* (Matthew 4:3).

Satan is also referred to as the "god of this world/age" (2 Corinthians 4:4), "prince of this world" (John 12:31), and "father of lies" (John 8:44).

---

1. Justin Martyr, *Dialogue of Justin philosopher and Martyr with Trypho, a Jew*, Chapter 103, The Pharisees are the bulls: the roaring lion is Herod or the devil ~156 AD.

Bodie Hodge is a speaker, writer, and researcher for Answers in Genesis. Bodie has a master's degree in mechanical engineering from Southern Illinois University at Carbondale. Since joining Answers in Genesis, Bodie has contributed to several books, including *Dragons: Legends and Lore of Dinosaurs*.

Was Satan Originally a Fallen Angel from Heaven?

by Bodie Hodge

Satan is mentioned in conjunction with angels (Matthew 25:41; Revelation 12:9) and the "sons of God" (Job 1:6, 2:1), which many believe to be angels. Although no Bible verse actually states that he was originally an angel, he is called a cherub in Ezekiel 28:16. The meaning of *cherub* is uncertain, though it is usually thought of as an angelic or heavenly being. (Ezekiel 28 is discussed in more detail later.)

In 2 Corinthians 11:14, we find that Satan masquerades as an angel of light—another allusion to his angel-like status: "And no wonder! For Satan himself transforms himself into an angel of light."

Although it is possible that Satan was an angel, it may be better to say that he was originally among the "heavenly host" since he came from heaven, but don't know with certainty that he was an actual angel (heavenly host would include angels). Recall Isaiah 14:12:

> How you are fallen from heaven, O Lucifer, son of the morning! How you are cut down to the ground, you who weakened the nations!

When Satan, the great dragon in Revelation 12:9 fell, it appears that he took a third of the heavenly host with him (a "third of the stars" were taken to earth with him by his tail, Revelation 12:4). Angels who fell have nothing good to look forward to:

Then He will also say to those on the left hand, "Depart from Me, you cursed, into the everlasting fire prepared for the devil and his angels . . ." (Matthew 25:41).

For if God did not spare the angels who sinned, but cast them down to hell and delivered them into chains of darkness, to be reserved for judgment . . . (2 Peter 2:4).

What these passages *don't* say is who and where the angels and Satan were originally.

And it grew up to the host of heaven; and it cast down some of the host and some of the stars to the ground, and trampled them (Daniel 8:10).

Daniel is speaking of heavenly hosts and angels, which were often spoken of as stars or luminaries (see Judges 5:20; Daniel 8:10; Jude 13; Revelation 1:20); it is unlikely that this passage refers to physical stars as such would destroy the earth. The Hebrew word for stars (*kowkab*) also includes planets, meteors, and comets. Were these stars, comets, and meteors? Likely not since the context refers to heavenly beings, which would be "trampled on." This is further confirmation that Satan (and perhaps some other heavenly host) and his angels sinned and fell.

Another key passage to this is Ezekiel 28:15–17 (discussed in more detail later). The passage indicates that Satan was indeed perfect before his fall. He was in heaven and was cast to the earth.

Were the Heavens, Satan, and His Angels Created?

Bodie Hodge

*T*he Bible doesn't give an *exact* time of Satan's creation or of his fall but does give some clues. Paul says in Colossians that *all things* were created by God/Christ:

> For by Him all things were created that are in heaven and that are on earth, visible and invisible, whether thrones or dominions or principalities or powers. All things were created through Him and for Him (Colossians 1:16).

So logically, Satan was created, as was the "heaven of heavens." Recall that Satan was originally in heaven prior to his fall. So the question becomes, when was the heaven of heavens created? The Bible uses the word *heaven* in several ways. The first mention is Genesis 1:1: "In the beginning God created the heavens and the earth."

The Hebrew word for heavens is plural, [*shamayim* dual of an unused singular *shameh*]. The word itself means heaven, heavens, sky, visible heavens, abode of stars, universe, atmosphere, and the abode of God. The context helps determine the meaning of a particular word; *heavens* is properly plural, and many Bible scholars and translators have rightly translated it as such.

Therefore, it seems safe to assume that the "heaven of heavens" was created along with the physical heavens (the space-time continuum, i.e., the physical universe, where the stars, sun, and moon would abide after they were created on Day 4) during Creation Week.

The definition of the Greek word for heaven(s) (*ouranos*) is similar: the vaulted expanse of the sky with all things visible in it;

the universe, the world; the aerial heavens or sky, the region where the clouds and the tempests gather, and where thunder and lightning are produced; the sidereal or starry heavens; the region above the sidereal heavens, the seat of order of things eternal and consummately perfect where God and other heavenly beings dwells.

By usage, this could include the heaven of heavens. However, other biblical passages also help to answer whether the heaven of heavens was created.

> You alone are the LORD; You have made heaven, the heaven of heavens, with all their host, the earth and everything on it, the seas and all that is in them, and You preserve them all. The host of heaven worships You (Nehemiah 9:6).

A clear distinction is made between at least two heavens—the physical heavens and the heaven of heavens. The physical heavens include the expanse made on Day 2, the place where the stars were placed on Day 4, and the atmosphere (birds are referred to as "of the air" and "of the heavens," e.g., 1 Kings 14:11; Job 12:7; Psalm 104:12). The heaven of heavens is the "residing place" (if such can be said) of the heavenly host, angels, and so on. This may be the third heaven which Paul mentions:

> I know a man in Christ who fourteen years ago—whether in the body I do not know, or out of the body I do not know, God knows—such a man was caught up to the third heaven (2 Corinthians 12:2).

The passage in Nehemiah indicates that God made the heavens; they are not infinite as God is. So the question now becomes, when?

Since the heaven of heavens is referred to with the earth, seas, and physical heaven, we can safely assume that they were all created during the same timeframe—during Creation Week. The creation of the heaven of heavens did not take place on Day 7, as God rested on that day from all of His work of creating. So it must have happened sometime during the six prior days.

Then God saw everything that He had made, and indeed it was very good. So the evening and the morning were the sixth day. Thus the heavens and the earth, and all the host of them, were finished (Genesis 1:31–2:1).

Everything that God made, whether on earth, sky, seas, or heaven, was "very good." Did this include the heaven of heavens and Satan and the angels? Absolutely! Satan is spoken of in Ezekiel 28:15:

> You were perfect in your ways from the day you were created, till iniquity was found in you.

This passage says that Satan was blameless, so he was *very good* originally. It would make sense then that the heaven of heavens was also a recipient of this blessed saying, since Satan was. In fact, this is what we would expect from an all-good God: a very good creation. Deuteronomy 32:4 says every work of God is perfect. So the heaven of heavens, Satan, and the angels were originally very good.

Ezekiel 28:15 says "from the *day*" (emphasis added) Satan was created. Obviously then, Satan had a beginning; he is not infinite as God is. Thus, Satan is bound to time. Other Scriptures also reveal the relationship between Satan and time:

> . . . Woe to the earth and the sea, because the devil has come down to you, having great wrath, knowing that he has only a short time (Revelation 12:12).

> When the devil had finished every temptation, he left Him until an opportune time (Luke 4:13).

As a created being with a beginning, Satan is bound by time. He is not omnipresent as God is, nor is he omniscient. God has declared the end from the beginning (Isaiah 46:10); Satan cannot.

We can be certain that Satan, the heaven of heavens, and all that is in them had a beginning.

When Were the Angels and Satan Created?

by Bodie Hodge

The Bible doesn't give the exact timing of the creation of Satan and the angels; however, several deductions can be made from Scripture concerning the timing. Consider Ezekiel 28:11–19:

¹¹ Moreover the word of the LORD came to me, saying,

¹² "Son of man, take up a lamentation for the king of Tyre, and say to him, 'Thus says the Lord GOD: "You were the seal of perfection, full of wisdom and perfect in beauty.

¹³ You were in Eden, the garden of God; every precious stone was your covering: the sardius, topaz, and diamond, beryl, onyx, and jasper, sapphire, turquoise, and emerald with gold. The workmanship of your timbrels and pipes was prepared for you on the day you were created.

¹⁴ You were the anointed cherub who covers; I established you; you were on the holy mountain of God; you walked back and forth in the midst of fiery stones.

¹⁵ You were perfect in your ways from the day you were created, till iniquity was found in you.

¹⁶ By the abundance of your trading you became filled with violence within, and you sinned; therefore I cast you as a profane thing out of the mountain of God; and I destroyed you, O covering cherub, from the midst of the fiery stones.

¹⁷ Your heart was lifted up because of your beauty; you corrupted your wisdom for the sake of your splendor; I cast

you to the ground, I laid you before kings, that they might gaze at you.

¹⁸ You defiled your sanctuaries by the multitude of your iniquities, by the iniquity of your trading; therefore I brought fire from your midst; it devoured you, and I turned you to ashes upon the earth in the sight of all who saw you.

¹⁹ All who knew you among the peoples are astonished at you; you have become a horror, and shall be no more forever."

In the sections prior to this, the word of the Lord was to Tyre itself (Ezekiel 27:2) and to the ruler of Tyre (Ezekiel 28:2). Beginning in Ezekiel 28:11, a lament (expression of grief or mourning for past events) is expressed to the king of Tyre; or more specifically, to the one *influencing* the king of Tyre. Note well that the king of Tyre was never a model of perfection (verse 12), nor was he on the mount of God (verse 14), nor was he in the Garden of Eden (verse 13; note that the Flood had destroyed the Garden of Eden several hundred years prior to this time period).

God easily sees Satan's influence and speaks directly to him. Elsewhere the Lord spoke to the serpent in Genesis 3. Genesis 3:14 is said to the serpent; Genesis 3:15 is said to Satan who influenced the serpent. Jesus rebuked Peter and then spoke to Satan (Mark 8:33). In Isaiah 14, the passage speaks to the King of Babylon and some parts to Satan, who was influencing him.

In the Ezekiel passage, we note that Satan was originally perfect (blameless) from the *day* he was created until he sinned (wickedness was found in him). Thus, it can be deduced that Satan was created during Creation Week; since he was blameless, he was under God's "very good" proclamation (Genesis 1:31) at the end of Day 6.

In Job 38:4–7, God spoke to Job:

> Where were you when I laid the foundations of the earth? Tell Me, if you have understanding. Who determined its measurements? Surely you know! Or who stretched the line upon

it? To what were its foundations fastened? Or who laid its cornerstone, when the morning stars sang together, and all the sons of God shouted for joy (Job 38:4–7)?

Although a poetic passage, it may tell us that some of God's creative work was eye witnessed by angels and that morning stars sang. Are morning stars symbolic of heavenly host or other angelic beings? It is possible—recall that stars are often equated with angelic or heavenly beings, and most commentators suggest this refers to angels.

If so, the creation of the angels was prior to Day 3 during Creation Week. From Genesis 1, God created the foundations of the earth on either Day 1 (earth created) or Day 3 (land and water separated). The logical inference is that the angels were created on either Day 1 or at least by Day 3.

If not, then the physical stars (created on Day 4) were present while the angels shouted for joy. If this was the case, then morning stars and angels did their singing and shouting after the stars were created.

It seems most likely that *morning stars* symbolize heavenly host or angels. Satan, one of the heavenly host, was called a morning star; therefore, Satan and the angels were created sometime prior to Day 3 (or early on Day 3), possibly on Day 1.

When did Satan fall?

Satan sinned when pride overtook him, and he fell from perfection (Ezekiel 28:15–17). When was this? The Bible doesn't give an exact answer, but deductions can again be made from the Scriptures:

How you are fallen from heaven, O Lucifer, son of the morning! How you are cut down to the ground, you who weakened the nations! For you have said in your heart: "I will ascend into heaven, I will exalt my throne above the stars of God; I will also sit on the mount of the congregation on the farthest sides of the north; I will ascend above the heights of the clouds, I will be like the Most High" (Isaiah 14:12–14).

When Satan sinned, he was cast from heaven (Isaiah 14:12). This must have been after Day 6 of Creation Week because God pronounced everything very good (Genesis 1:31). Otherwise, God would have pronounced Satan's rebellion very good; yet throughout Scripture, God is absolute that sin is detestable in His eyes.

God sanctified the seventh day. It seems unlikely that God would have sanctified a day in which a great rebellion occurred. In Genesis 1:28 God commanded Adam and Eve to be fruitful and multiply. Had they waited very long to have sexual relations, they would have been sinning against God by not being fruitful. So, it couldn't have been long after Day 7 that Satan tempted the woman through the serpent.

Archbishop Ussher, the great seventeenth-century Bible scholar, placed Satan's fall on the tenth day of the first year, which is representative of the Day of Atonement. The Day of Atonement reflected back to the sin and sacrifice, including the first sacrifice when God made coverings for Adam and Eve from the coats of animal skins (Genesis 3:21). It may be that the generations that followed (from Abel to Noah to Abraham to the Israelites) mimicked this pattern of sacrificing for sins on the Day of Atonement. Regardless, the fall of Satan would likely have been soon after Day 7.

Some have claimed that Satan's fall was between Genesis 1:1 and Genesis 1:2. This is popularly called the *gap theory* which was popularized by Scottish theologian Thomas Chalmers in the 1800s while trying to accommodate the secular view of fossil and rock layers that the secularists claim is "millions of years" into the Bible.[1] Gap theorists try to make the case that the Hebrew in Genesis 1:2 should be translated as "And the earth *became* without form, and void" and this is subsequent to Satan's fall.

However, recognized grammarians, lexicographers, and linguists have almost uniformly rejected the translations "became" and "had become." It is a basic exegetical fallacy to claim that because *Strong's Concordance* lists "became" as one of the meanings of *haya* (Hebrew word used for "was"), it is legitimate to translate it this way in the particular context of Genesis 1:2. It is simply grammatically impossible when the verb *haya* is combined with a *waw* disjunctive—in the rest of the Old Testament, *Waw* + a noun + *haya* (qal perfect, 3rd person) is always translated, "was" or "came," but *never* "became."

Further, Moses also makes it very clear (e.g., Exodus 20:11, 31:17) that *all things* were created in six actual days.[2] Additionally, the idea that there were life forms, which we find in the fossils, that lived *and died* prior to the creation of Adam or the animals and the subsequent entrance of sin into the world undermines the gospel and denigrates the character of God.

When He was finished creating, God looked at His completed creation and called it "very good" (Genesis 1:31). Accepting "millions of years" of prior life forms that we find in the fossil layers living and dying (and suffering from terrible diseases such as cancer or brain tumors) means that God labeled this process "good." But can we honestly think death (and disease, pain, and suffering) is good?

Paul describes death as an *enemy* (1 Corinthians 15:26), and John tells us that it has no place in the new heavens and earth (Revelation 21:4). In fact, death was Adam's punishment for disobeying God (Genesis 2:17, 3:19; Romans 5:12). If Adam's punishment was *very good*, then why didn't he eat from the tree of knowledge of good and evil right away? And why would Jesus Christ come and die in our place to save us from death if death were a "very good" process that had been occurring for billions of years?

Two ways of looking at the rock layers.

Millions of years of rock and fossil layers virtually disappear in light of the global Flood in Genesis 6–8, which is the cause for the bulk of the fossil and rock layers. If one accepts the fossil and rock

Death after Sin

God's Word
Is Truth

Death for
Millions of Years

Man Decides
Truth

layers as representing millions of years then they are trusting man's ideas about the past over God's Word, which reveals the past. It is better to stand on the authority of the Word of God that doesn't change, as opposed to the changing ideas of man about the past.

Consider Jesus's words in Mark 10:6 when asked about marriage and divorce. Jesus responded, "But at the beginning of creation God made them male and female."

If the world really were billions of years old and man just showed up recently, then Jesus would be wrong—He should have said "*near the end* of creation." But since the world was only about 4,000 years old when Jesus said this, and He had created man and woman on Day 6 (only five days after "the beginning"), then Jesus was correct. Jesus believed in a young earth, not the "gap theory," so there is no reason for us to accept this unbiblical idea.[3]

When did Adam and Eve rebel?

In Genesis 1:28, God commanded Adam and Eve to be fruitful and multiply. If they had waited very long, they would have been sinning against God by not being fruitful. Also, since they were created with perfect bodies, it would not have taken long for Eve to conceive. So, the time between the Creation and the Fall must have been short.

Some people have said that the Fall could not have occurred so early because Adam walked with God in the Garden and this suggests an intimate relationship between Adam and His Creator that could only be developed *over time*. However, the Bible never says that Adam walked with God in the Garden. Although many people have taught this, it is not found in Scripture. Adam and Eve were hiding because of their sin when they heard the sound of the Lord God walking in the Garden (Genesis 3:8), and note that this is *after* sin.

In Genesis 3, Adam and Eve sinned and were kicked out of the Garden of Eden. According to Scripture, this happened prior to conceiving their first child, Cain (Genesis 4:1).

Genesis 5:3 indicates that Adam had Seth at age 130, and Genesis 4:25 indicates this took place after Cain killed Abel. Adam had at least three children before Seth: Cain (Genesis 4:1), Cain's wife[4] (Genesis 4:17), and Abel (Genesis 4:2). Since Cain and Abel were old enough to work with crops and herds, respectively, the maximum time before the Fall would have to be much less than 130 years.

Looking back at the Creation Week, Adam and Eve couldn't have sinned on Day 6 (the day Adam and the Woman were created), since God declared that everything was "very good." Otherwise, sin would be very good. Day 7 is also unlikely, since God sanctified that day. Therefore, the Fall likely happened soon after this.

Archbishop Ussher suggests that Adam sinned on the tenth day of the first month in Ussher's chronology, which is the Day of Atonement.[5] The Day of Atonement presumably represents the first sacrifice, which God made by killing animals (from which He made coats of skins in Genesis 3:21) to cover Adam and Eve's sin.

Ussher's reasons for choosing this date make sense. However, we can't be certain of the exact date or length of time prior to the Fall beyond the points established above.

How long ago was the Curse?

The Curse would have been fairly soon after the creation of Adam and Eve on Day 6 because it didn't take long for them to sin (see When Did Adam and Eve Rebel? below) We can do a basic calculation to arrive at the date of creation and Adam's creation. The Curse must have been close to the same time. So, let's calculate the date of creation.

Adam was created on Day 6, so there were 5 days before him. If we add up the dates from Adam to Abraham, we get about 2,000 years, using the Masoretic Hebrew text (which is the standard Hebrew text that most English translations are based on) of Genesis 5 and 11.[6] Whether Christian or secular, most scholars would agree that Abraham lived about 2000 BC (4,000 years ago).

So, a simple calculation is:

$$
\begin{array}{r}
5 \text{ days} \\
+ \sim 2{,}000 \text{ years} \\
+ \sim 4{,}000 \text{ years} \\
\hline
\sim 6{,}000 \text{ years}
\end{array}
$$

At this point, the first five days are negligible. Quite a few people have done this calculation using the Masoretic text and, with careful attention to the biblical details, arrived at the same time frame of about 6,000 years, or about 4000 BC. Two of the most popular, and perhaps the best, are a recent work by Dr. Floyd Jones and a much earlier book by Archbishop James Ussher (1581–1656):

Table 1: Table of Jones and Ussher

Who?	Creation Date Calculated	Reference and Date
Archbishop James Ussher	4004 BC	*The Annals of the World*, AD 1658
Dr. Floyd Nolan Jones	4004 BC	*The Chronology of the Old Testament*, AD 1993

Often there is a misconception that Ussher and Jones were the only ones to do a chronology and arrive at an age of about 6,000 years. However, this is not the case. Jones gives a listing of several chronologists who undertook the task of calculating the age of the earth based on the Bible, and their calculations range from 5501 to 3836 BC. A few are listed in Table 2.

Table 2: Chronologists' calculations according to Dr. Jones

	Chronologist	When Calculated?	Date BC
1	Julius Africanus	c. 240	5501
2	George Syncellus	c. 810	5492
3	John Jackson	1752	5426
4	Dr William Hales	c. 1830	5411
5	Eusebius	c. 330	5199
6	Marianus Scotus	c. 1070	4192
7	L. Condomanus	n/a	4141
8	Thomas Lydiat	c. 1600	4103
9	M. Michael Maestlinus	c. 1600	4079
10	J. Ricciolus	n/a	4062
11	Jacob Salianus	c. 1600	4053
12	H. Spondanus	c. 1600	4051
13	Martin Anstey	1913	4042

	Chronologist	When Calculated?	Date BC
14	W. Lange	n/a	4041
15	E. Reinholt	n/a	4021
16	J. Cappellus	c. 1600	4005
17	E. Greswell	1830	4004
18	E. Faulstich	1986	4001
19	D. Petavius	c. 1627	3983
20	Frank Klassen	1975	3975
21	Becke	n/a	3974
22	Krentzeim	n/a	3971
23	W. Dolen	2003	3971
24	E. Reusnerus	n/a	3970
25	J. Claverius	n/a	3968
26	C. Longomontanus	c. 1600	3966
27	P. Melanchthon	c. 1550	3964
28	J. Haynlinus	n/a	3963
29	A. Salmeron	d. 1585	3958
30	J. Scaliger	d. 1609	3949
31	M. Beroaldus	c. 1575	3927
32	A. Helwigius	c. 1630	3836

As you will note from Table 2, the dates are not all 4004 BC. There are two primary reasons chronologists have varying dates:[7]

1. Some used the Septuagint or another early translation instead of the Hebrew Masoretic text. The Septuagint is a Greek translation of the Hebrew Old Testament done around 250 BC by about 70 Jewish scholars (which is why it is often called the LXX, the Roman numeral for 70). While good in most places, there are a

number of inaccuracies. For example, one relates to the Genesis chronologies in which the LXX calculations would have Methuselah living beyond the Flood—without being on the Ark!

2. Several points in the biblical time line are not straightforward to calculate. They require very careful study of more than one passage. These include exactly how much time the Israelites were in Egypt and what Terah's age was when Abraham was born. (See Jones's and Ussher's books for a detailed discussion of these difficulties.)

The first four in Table 2 have much higher dates and are calculated from the Septuagint, which gives ages for the patriarchs' firstborn much higher than the Masoretic text or the Samarian Pentateuch (another version from the Jews in Samaria just before Christ). Because of this, the LXX adds in extra time. Though the Samarian and Masoretic texts are much closer, they still have a couple of differences.

Table 3: Septuagint, Masoretic, and Samarian early patriarchal ages

Name	Masoretic	Samarian Pentateuch	Septuagint
Adam	130	130	230
Seth	105	105	205
Enosh	90	90	190
Cainan	70	70	170
Mahalaleel	65	65	165
Jared	162	62	162
Enoch	65	65	165
Methuselah	187	67	167
Lamech	182	53	188
Noah	500	500	500

Using data from Table 2 (excluding the Septuagint calculations and including Jones and Ussher), the average date of the creation of the earth is: 4045 BC. This yields an average of about 6,000 years for the time of the Curse.

The world has been enduring the results of the Curse for 6,000 years and there are still many remnants of beauty and wonder. Just imagine what it was like before sin and what believers can look forward to in the new heavens and new earth where there is no more Curse!

1. W. Hanna, ed., *Natural Theology*, Selected works of Thomas Chalmers, Vol. 5, Thomas Constable, Edinburgh, 1857, 146. The only thing Chalmers basically states concerning the gap theory in these writings is "The detailed history of creation in the first chapter of Genesis begins at the middle of the second verse."

2. For a more detailed analysis of the days of creation please see: Ham, Ken, *The New Answers Book*, Chapter 8: Could God have really created everything in six days?, Master Books, Green Forest, Arkansas, 2006.

3. For a more detailed analysis on the gap theory, please see: Ham, Ken, *The New Answers Book*, Chapter 5: What about gap and ruin-reconstruction theories?, Master Books, Green Forest, Arkansas, 2006.

4. Although we cannot be certain that Cain's wife was his sister (it could have been a niece, etc.), either way a brother or sister would have had to originally be married to have offspring if it were a niece, great niece, etc.

5. Archbishop James Ussher, *The Annals of the World*, translated by Larry and Marion Pierce (Master Books: Green Forest, Arkansas, 2003), p. 18.

6. Bodie Hodge, "Ancient Patriarch in Genesis," Answers in Genesis website, January 20, 2009, http://www.answersingenesis.org/articles/2009/01/20/ancient-patriarchs-in-genesis.

7. Other reasons include gaps in the chronology based on the presences of an extra Cainan in Luke 3:36. But there are good reasons this should be left out. It is included in late copies of the Septuagint (LXX). But early copies of the LXX do not have it, so it was added later. The 18th-century Hebrew expert John Gill points out: "This Cainan is not mentioned by Moses in Genesis 11:12 nor has he ever appeared in any Hebrew copy of the Old Testament, nor in the Samaritan version, nor in the Targum; nor is he mentioned by Josephus, nor in 1Chronicles 1:24 where the genealogy is repeated; nor is it in Beza's most ancient Greek copy of Luke: it indeed stands in the present copies of the Septuagint, but was not originally there; and therefore could not be taken by Luke from thence, but seems to be owing to some early negligent transcriber of Luke's Gospel, and since put into the Septuagint to give it authority: I say 'early,' because it is in many Greek copies, and in the Vulgate Latin, and all the Oriental versions, even in the Syriac, the oldest of them; but ought not to stand neither in the text, nor in any version: for certain it is, there never was such a Cainan, the son of Arphaxad, for Salah was his son; and with him the next words should be connected."

How Could Satan, Who Was Created Good, Become Evil?

by Bodie Hodge

From what we can tell from studying the Bible, Satan was the first to sin. He sinned before the woman sinned, and before Adam sinned. Some claim that we sin because Satan enters us and causes us to sin, but the Bible doesn't teach this. We sin whether Satan would enter or not. Satan was influencing the serpent when the woman sinned and when Adam sinned; they sinned on their own accord without being able to claim that "Satan made me do it."

But what caused this initial sin, why did Satan sin in the first place?

> Let no one say when he is tempted, "I am tempted by God"; for God cannot be tempted by evil, nor does He Himself tempt anyone. But each one is tempted when he is drawn away by his own desires and enticed. Then, when desire has conceived, it gives birth to sin; and sin, when it is full-grown, brings forth death (James 1:13–15).

Death is the punishment for sin. Sin originates in desire— one's *own* desire. It was by Satan's own desire that his pride in his own beauty and abilities overtook him.

In the "very good" original creation, Satan and mankind had the power of contrite choice.[1] In the Garden of Eden, the woman was convinced by her own *desire* (the tree was *desirable* to make one wise—Genesis 3:6). Satan had not entered her; she was enticed by her own desire.

God is not the author of sin; our desires are. God did not trick or deceive Satan into becoming full of pride. God hates pride (Proverbs 8:13), and it would not be in His character to cause one to become prideful. Nor was He the one who deceived Eve. Deception and lies go hand in hand (Psalm 78:36; Proverbs 12:17), yet God does not lie or deceive (Titus 1:2; Hebrews 6:18).

Note that since Satan's *own desires* caused his pride, the blame for evil's entrance into creation cannot be attributed to God. To clarify, this doesn't mean God was unaware this would happen, but God permitted it to happen. God is sovereign and acted justly by using Michael and his angels to cast Satan out of heaven after he rebelled against the Creator (Revelation 12:7–9).

Therefore, when God-incarnate came to destroy evil and the work of the devil (1 John 3:8), it was truly an act of love, not a gimmick to correct what some falsely claim He "messed up." God was glorified in His plan for redemption.

Some have asked why God didn't send Satan to hell instead of casting him to earth, assuming this would have prevented death, suffering, or curses for mankind. But God is love, and this shows that God was patient with him as God is patient with us. Perhaps Satan would have had a possibility of salvation had he not continued in his rebellion and sealed his fate, although Genesis 3:15 revealed that Satan's head would be crushed (after his continued sin and deception of the woman).

A related question could be, "Was Satan required for man to sin? Satan's temptation of the woman instigated her to look at the fruit of the tree of the knowledge of good and evil, but it was she who *desired* it and sinned. Can we really say with certainty that on another day, without Satan, the woman and/or Adam would not have desired the fruit and sinned? However, in the words of Aslan, the lion in C. S. Lewis's *Chronicles of Narnia*, "there are no what-ifs."

In reality, we suffer death and the Curse because Adam sinned (Genesis 3), and we sinned in Adam (Hebrews 7:9–10) and continue to sin (Romans 5:12). Adam did his part, but we must take responsibility for our part in committing high treason against the Creator of the universe. It is faulty to think that death and suffering are the result of Satan's rebellion.

Man had dominion over the world, and Satan did not (Genesis 1:26–28). When Satan rebelled, the world wasn't cursed; when Adam sinned, the ground was cursed, death entered the world, and so on. This is why we needed a last Adam (1 Corinthians 15:45), not a "last Eve" or "last Satan." This is why Christ came. The good news is that for those in Christ, the punishment for sin (death) will have no sting (1 Corinthians 15:55), and they will have eternal life.

1.　Whether mankind had this power after the Fall has been an extensive debate within the church for hundreds of years, and is not for discussion in this book.

What Will Become of Satan?

by Bodie Hodge

Satan's days are numbered, and he will be condemned eternally.

> Therefore rejoice, O heavens, and you who dwell in them! Woe to the inhabitants of the earth and the sea! For the devil has come down to you, having great wrath, because he knows that he has a short time (Revelation 12:12).

> And he cast him into the bottomless pit, and shut him up, and set a seal on him, so that he should deceive the nations no more till the thousand years were finished. But after these things he must be released for a little while (Revelation 20:3).

We should have no fear of Satan or his minions since God has power over him and has already decreed what his outcome will be—a second death—an eternal punishment called hell.

> Then He will also say to those on the left hand, "Depart from Me, you cursed, into the everlasting fire prepared for the devil and his angels . . ." (Matthew 25:41).

> The devil, who deceived them, was cast into the lake of fire and brimstone where the beast and the false prophet are. And they will be tormented day and night forever and ever (Revelation 20:10).

> Then Death and Hades were cast into the lake of fire. This is the second death (Revelation 20:14).

Some people may claim that they want to "rule with Satan in hell," rather than go to heaven and enjoy the infinite goodness of God. Sadly, these people fail to realize that Satan has *no* power in hell, nor will they. Satan is not the "ruler" in hell but a captive just as they will be if they don't receive the free gift of eternal life by repenting of their sins and believing in the finished work of Jesus Christ on the Cross.

There will be nothing good in hell, no friendships, no companionships, no love, etc. Good things come from a good God. And hell, is separation from God, and likewise, separation from all good things.

We trust those reading this book will realize that the only way of salvation is found through a personal, saving belief in Jesus Christ. God has provided a way of salvation, a right relationship with Him, and a means of forgiveness; have you received Christ as your Savior?

Did the Serpent Originally Have Legs?

by Bodie Hodge

Perhaps one of the most-asked and most-debated topics is the serpent's original appearance. One of the early models of the serpent at the Answers in Genesis Creation Museum (just outside of Cincinnati, Ohio) is pictured at left for you to consider.

Determining features of the serpent from the precious little information given in the Bible is a difficult task, and there is considerable speculation in this area. For example, we can speculate about what color and patterns were on the serpent's exterior, what shape of eyes the serpent had, and so on.

What does the Bible say?

Even the question of legs on the serpent is one with varying speculation. Consider the biblical text to see what it says of the serpent:

> Now the serpent was more cunning than any beast of the field which the LORD God had made. And he said to the woman, "Has God indeed said, 'You shall not eat of every tree of the garden'?"

> And the woman said to the serpent, "We may eat the fruit of the trees of the garden; but of the fruit of the tree which is in the midst of the garden, God has said, 'You shall not eat it, nor shall you touch it, lest you die.'"

> Then the serpent said to the woman, "You will not surely

die. For God knows that in the day you eat of it your eyes will be opened, and you will be like God, knowing good and evil" (Genesis 3:1–5).

And the LORD God said to the woman, "What is this you have done?" The woman said, "The serpent deceived me, and I ate."

So the LORD God said to the serpent: "Because you have done this, you are cursed more than all cattle, and more than every beast of the field; on your belly you shall go, and you shall eat dust all the days of your life. And I will put enmity between you and the woman, and between your seed and her Seed; He shall bruise your head, and you shall bruise His heel" (Genesis 3:13–15).

According to Genesis 3:13–15, there is no direct indication that the serpent had legs, only that its curse would be "on your belly you shall go." But in Genesis 3:1, we get a clue that the serpent was likely classified as a beast of the field, which is probably why beasts of the field were also mentioned in 3:14.[1]

What makes this an issue is that it was a *land* animal and/or flying reptile in general—hence, it moved by flying, slithering, or with appendages. If it slithered already, what was the point of the curse, and why compare it to creatures which had legs in Genesis 3:14?

Regardless if it was a beast of the field, the serpent was indeed a land animal and capable of locomotion in the Garden of Eden and in the field. Let's evaluate forms of locomotion to see the possibilities.

Locomotion

Land animals are currently known to have three classes of locomotion:[2]

- Legged (or some form of appendages)

- Slithering

- Rolling

Beasts of the field, and virtually all land animals, use leg(s) to move, from cattle as a quadruped to inch worms, which use two grabbing spots on their body to inch along. Of course, snakes and legless lizards slither.

The other means of locomotion is rolling. Few creatures today roll, and of these creatures, the rolling is only temporary. The primary means is using gravity and balling up to roll down a hill, like a web-toed salamander or a Namid wheeling spider.

Few land animals have a self-powered rolling mechanism. There are two that come to mind, mother-of-pearl moth caterpillar stage and the Pangolins both use a leg(s) and/or tail with which to push. But even these rolling creatures use some form of appendage or leg; so, arguably, there are really only two types of locomotion found among land animals today: slithering or legged.

Was there some other form of locomotion among creatures that are now extinct? Without further research, there is no certain answer.

As for the possibility of wings, this can't be entirely ruled out either. But if so, then the serpent had some form of locomotion other than slithering and some form of appendage that physically changed forms.

Hebrew and Greek

The Hebrew word for *serpent* is *nachash,* and the Greek equivalent is *ophis.* It means "snake, serpent, sly, cunning, and image of a serpent." The late Dr. Henry Morris says of the Hebrew word:

> There has been much speculation as to whether the serpent originally was able to stand upright (the Hebrew word

nachash, some maintain, originally meant "shining, upright creature").[3]

Although, this speculated meaning may have been deduced from Genesis 3:14 regarding the serpent being forced to crawl on its belly, this doesn't really help us ascertain if the serpent had legs or not.

Commentaries

Several commentaries were checked to see what other scholars said about the serpent. They are accumulated below. Of course, commentaries are not inspired like the Bible is, but they can give us some insight.

Table 1: Commentaries and the Serpent's Appearance[4]

Commentator(s)	Legs/physical change?
Henry Morris	Yes
John Gill	Yes (whether feet or flying)
Matthew Henry	Yes (perhaps feet and wings)
John Calvin	No
Adam Clarke	Yes
Leupold	Yes/No—open to both—not necessarily a complete transformation but leans toward few, if any changes
Matthew Poole	Yes
John Trapp	Yes
Martin Luther	Yes
Allen P. Ross	Yes
C.F. Keil and F. Delitzsch	Yes
Flavius Josephus	Yes
Gordon Wenham	No
John Sailhamer	No

Most commentaries seem certain that it was referring to some form of erect creature and that changes took place with the curse. John Calvin was the only one of these who seemed to think that the serpent remained with the same form.[5] He said that the curse was more of a statement to "put the serpent back in its place." Leupold leaves open either position but leans against a full transformation, leaving the serpent more in its original form. Wenham and Sailhamer more recently (1987 and 1990 respectively) both lean against the serpent changing forms but give no reasons why they believe this.

The problem with leaving the serpent "as is" is that it reduces the curse to almost a meaningless status. If such a philosophy is to be held, then the parallel comments by the Lord to the woman and the man should also be statements to just "put them back in their place." This raises theological issues. It would mean that the other effects of sin listed in Genesis 3, such as thorns and thistles, increased pain and sorrow for the woman, and mankind returning to dust, were merely statements to put human beings back in their place, not real changes. This seems highly illogical, as it would have death before sin in humans, with man already returning to dust (recall Romans 5:12).

Conclusion

The more logical answer is that the serpent originally had some form of legs or appendages, and these were either lost or reduced (consider how many reptiles crawl on their bellies and yet have legs, e.g., crocodiles). This seems to correlate with the plainest reading of the passage and the comparison of a curse ("on your belly you shall go") as compared with cattle and other beasts of the field, which do have legs.

Thorns and thistles were brought forth due to the curse (physical changes to vegetation); there were physical changes to the man and woman (increased sorrow in childbearing and increased pain in work that has been passed along). There is no reason to assume the serpent didn't undergo physical changes as well—he was a prime culprit. These physical changes due to the curse help explain certain defense and attack structures (DAS) in animals and plants that currently dominate the world.

---

1.   I personally lean toward the serpent being a beast of the field (not dogmatically), as I understand that it could simply be compared to them in the same way we can compare a bird to the beasts of the field.

2.   This excludes motion by gliding such as flying squirrels. Such locomotion is only temporary for land animals, and they have other means of movement while on the land. Note that we do not include birds as "land animals" although they live and reproduce on land or in trees (this is due to the biblical distinction that birds were created on Day 5 and not Day 6).

3.   Henry Morris, *The Genesis Record* (Baker Book House, 1976), p. 108.

4.   For references, see the online version of this chapter at answersingenesis.org/genesis/garden-of-eden/did-the-serpent-originally-have-legs/

5.   From several statements made by Calvin, this is the impression of the author regarding Calvin's point of view, although it is not 100% clear that he believed that the change to be only temporary.

Shouldn't Eve Have Been Shocked that a Serpent Spoke?

by Bodie Hodge

Often, people say that they can't believe the serpent in Genesis 3 spoke because they claim animals don't speak! Well, I wish I could tell that to my sister-in-law's Blue-Fronted Amazon Parrot that doesn't stop talking! Many types of parrots talk by mimicking, so it would be illogical to think that God didn't give this ability to other animals—especially in a perfect world.

Speaking human-sounding words and speaking intelligently, however, is not the same. Balaam's donkey, as the only other example given of animals speaking in Scripture, was specially enabled by the power of God to speak intelligently to Balaam. Because there is no other place in Scripture that reveals Satan or demons can cause animals to speak, it makes more sense that the serpent could make the sounds capable of speech, and Satan used this to his advantage. In essence, Satan likely used this feature that the original serpent had and caused it to say what he wanted.

Although this may *sound* farfetched, there should be caution about limiting what God did or didn't do in the perfect Garden. There is a possibility that many other animals had the ability to "speak" before the Curse. Many animals have types of sound-based or mimicry forms of communication today.

But the serpent was "clever" when it spoke. It made sense to the Woman.[1] Since Satan was the one who influenced the serpent

(Revelation 12:9, 20:2), then it makes sense why the serpent could deliver a cogent message capable of deceiving her. The serpent apparently cooperated and was an instrument in the deception and so deserved a punishment, which God justly gave. This reminds me of Judas, who also received due punishment, even though Satan entered him (Luke 22:3).

Of course today, serpents don't speak, but the Curse in Genesis 3:14 probably had something to do with this. Recall the physical changes in Genesis 3. Perhaps this is the reason the particular kind of serpent that deceived the Woman did not pass along the ability to speak or may have even become extinct since the Fall.[2]

The issue of the Woman being *shocked* when she heard the serpent speak also has a couple of problems. First, everything in the Garden of Eden was new to the first couple—they'd only been alive for a short time. Even a bug, cat, or dinosaur would all be new, so they wouldn't have been shocked at a talking serpent.

God also programmed language into Adam and Eve (since they were able to speak immediately with God), which would have included some words that describe animals and their capabilities. So it shouldn't have been *shocking* to see or hear something for the first time if you're already "programmed" to know about something like talking animals.

---

1.   When using "Woman" in caps, this denotes Eve's original name as given in Genesis 2:23, when Adam named her. She was originally named Woman and it seems she wasn't given the name Eve until after sin. Throughout these chapters both names are used. Most of the time they are corresponding to the name prior to and after sin but not always. The use of the names "Man" and "Adam" were both used prior to sin for the first man. So, sometimes one may see Adam and the Woman referenced, so please note that the name Woman is not used in any derogatory sense, but simply as a name.

2.   There were no land-dwelling, air-breathing animal kinds extinct by the time of the Flood since representatives of *each* kind were aboard the Ark (Genesis 6:19–20). If this were a particular serpent kind that went extinct, it would have been after the Flood.

Was Satan the Actual Serpent in the Garden?

by Bodie Hodge

This interpretation primarily comes from Revelation 12:9 and 20:2 without much regard to other passages, such as Genesis 3.

> So the great dragon was cast out, that serpent of old, called the devil and Satan, who deceives the whole world; he was cast to the earth, and his angels were cast out with him (Revelation 12:9).

> He laid hold of the dragon, that serpent of old, who is the devil and Satan, and bound him for a thousand years (Revelation 20:2).

These verses give excellent information about Satan and his many names as well as his involvement back in Eden, being the serpent of old. But does this eliminate that he used a real serpent? Not necessarily. The whole of Scripture needs to be consulted.

We read in Genesis 3 that there was a real serpent, and it received a real, physical curse to crawl on its belly and eat dust for the duration of its life (Genesis 3:14). Satan is not a physical being, although he can operate in the physical realm (Job 1–2). He is a spiritual being that operates in the spiritual realm as evidenced in many passages that detail his spiritual attributes, such as 1 Peter 5:8; Matthew 16:23; Acts 5:3; and Ephesians 6:12.

> Behold My hands and My feet, that it is I Myself. Handle Me and see, for a spirit does not have flesh and bones as you see I have (Luke 24:39).

The Bible seems to portray Satan and his angels as disembodied spirits. So then, how can both Satan and a real serpent be the culprit? From other passages, we find an important principle. Satan and demons can enter into people and animals and influence them. For example, Judas was entered by Satan in Luke 22:3; Peter was influenced by Satan[1] (Matthew 16:23); and the swine were entered by Legion, which consisted of many demons (Mark 5; Matthew 8).

Although such things may escape us, God easily sees when Satan is influencing someone and will often speak directly to Satan. Beginning in Ezekiel 28:11, for example, God is speaking to Satan who was influencing the King of Tyre. In the sections prior to this, the *Word of the Lord* was said to Tyre itself (Ezekiel 27:2), then to the ruler of Tyre (Ezekiel 28:2), and now *a lament* (expression of grief or mourning for past events) beginning in Ezekiel 28:11 to the King of Tyre. This one specifically was directed to the one influencing the King of Tyre—Satan—since the person, the King of Tyre, was never a model of perfection, nor was he on the mount of God, nor was he in the Garden of Eden, nor was he perfect in his ways from the day he was created, till iniquity was found in him (v. 15).

In Isaiah 14, the passage speaks to the King of Babylon and in some parts to Satan, who was influencing him. In Scripture, God sometimes speaks both to the person and to the one influencing that person—Satan.

So there is no stretch to understand that the Lord is speaking to the serpent and Satan in Genesis 3. Genesis 3:14 is said to the serpent and then Genesis 3:15 is said to Satan who is influencing the serpent. Martin Luther states it this way:

> Let us therefore, establish in the first place that the serpent is a real serpent, but one that has been entered and taken over by Satan.[2]

The Bible tells us that Satan used a real serpent to deceive Eve. And because of his entrance into the serpent, he can rightly be called the "serpent of old" or "great dragon" in Revelation.

---

1.   This was prior to the outpouring/indwelling of the Holy Spirit for Christians, which does away with the possibility of demonic or Satanic possession in Christians (1 Corinthians 6:19–20; Luke 11:21).

2.   Martin Luther, *Luther's Works*, vol. 1, ed. Jaroslav Pelikan (St. Louis, MO: Concordia Publishing House, 1958), p. 185.

Who Sinned First—
Adam or Satan?

by Bodie Hodge

When Christians speak of Adam being the first sinner, this refers to Paul saying,

> Therefore, just as through one man sin entered into the world, and death through sin, and so death spread to all men, because all sinned (Romans 5:12).

It means that sin *entered* the world through Adam—that is, Adam is the one credited with sin's entrance and hence the subsequent entrance of death and suffering and the need for a Savior and a last Adam (1 Corinthians 15:45). When we look back at Genesis 3, it is true that Satan had rebelled and also the Woman (later named Eve) sinned prior to Adam.

The sin of the Woman (Eve)

There were several things that Eve did wrong prior to eating the fruit. The first was her misspeaking while responding to the serpent. When the serpent (who was speaking the words of Satan) asked in Genesis 3:1: "Has God indeed said, 'You shall not eat of every tree of the garden?'" her response was less than perfect:

> And the woman said to the serpent, "We may eat the fruit of the trees of the garden; but of the fruit of the tree which is in the midst of the garden, God has said, 'You shall not eat it, *nor shall you touch it*, lest you die'" (Genesis 3:2–3; emphasis added).

Compare this to what God had commanded in Genesis 2:16–17:

> And the LORD God commanded the man, saying, "Of every tree of the garden you may freely eat; but of the tree of the knowledge of good and evil you shall not eat, for in the day that you eat of it you shall surely die."

The Woman made four mistakes in her response:

1. She added the command not to *touch* the fruit ("Nor shall you touch it"). This may even be in contradiction with the command to tend the Garden (Genesis 2:15), which may have necessitated touching the tree and the fruit from time to time. This also makes the command from God to seem exceptionally harsh.

2. She amended that God allowed them to *freely* eat. This makes God out to be less gracious.

3. She amended that God allowed them to freely eat from *every* tree. Again, this makes God out to be less gracious.

4. She amended the meaning of die. The Hebrew in Genesis 2:17 is "die-die" (*muwth-muwth*), which is often translated as "surely die" or literally as "dying you shall die," which indicates the beginning of dying, an ingressive sense. In other words, if they would have eaten the fruit, then Adam and Eve would have *begun to die* and would return to dust (which is what happened when they ate in Genesis 3:19). If they were meant to die right then, Genesis 2:17 should have used *muwth* only once as is used in the Hebrew meaning "dead," "died," or "die" in an absolute sense and not *beginning to* die or *surely* die as die-die is commonly used. What Eve said was "die" (*muwth*) once instead of the way God said it in Genesis 2:17 as "die-die" (*muwth-muwth*). So, she changed God's Word to appear harsher again by saying they would die almost immediately.

Often we are led to believe that Satan merely deceived Eve with the statement, "You will not surely die" in Genesis 3:4. But we neglect the cleverness/cunningness that God indicates the serpent had in Genesis 3:1. Note also that the exchange seems to suggest that Eve may have been willingly led; that is, she had already changed what God had said.

If you take a closer look, the serpent argued against Eve with an extremely clever ploy. He went back and argued against her incorrect words using the correct phraseology that God used in Genesis 2:17 ("die-die" [*muwth-muwth*]). This, in a deceptive way, used the proper sense of die that God stated in Genesis 2:17 against Eve's mistaken view. Imagine the conversation in simplified terms like this:

> **God says**: Don't eat, or you will begin to die.
> **Eve says**: We can't eat, or we will die *immediately*.
> **Serpent says**: You will not *begin* to die.

This was very clever of Satan. This is not an isolated incident either. When Satan tried tempting Jesus (Matthew 4), Jesus said "it is written" and quoted Scripture (Matthew 4:4). The second time Satan tried quoting Scripture (i.e. God) but did it deceptively just as he had done to Eve (Matthew 4:5–6). Of course, Jesus was not deceived, but corrected Satan's twisted use of Scripture (Matthew 4:7). But because of Eve's mistaken view of God's Word, it was easier for her to be deceived by Satan's misuse of Scripture.

From there, she started down the slope into sin by being enticed by the fruit (James 1:14–15). This culminated with eating the forbidden fruit and giving some to her husband and encouraging him to eat. Eve sinned against God by eating the fruit from the tree of the knowledge of good and evil prior to Adam. However, with a closer look at the text, their eyes were not opened until after Adam ate—likely only moments later (Genesis 3:7). Since Adam was created first (Eve coming from him, but both being created in God's image) and had been given the command directly, it required his sin to bring about the Fall of mankind. When Adam ate and sinned, they knew something was wrong and felt ashamed (Genesis 3:7). Sin and death had entered into the creation.

The sin of Satan

Like Eve, Satan had sinned prior to this. His sin was pride in his beauty (Ezekiel 28:15–17) while in a perfect heaven (Isaiah 14:12), and he was cast out when imperfection was found in him (Isaiah 14:12; Revelation 12:9; Ezekiel 28:15). Then we found him in the Garden of Eden (Ezekiel 28:13; Genesis 3).

Unlike Adam, Satan was not created in the image of God and was never given dominion over the world (Genesis 1:28). So, his sin did not affect the creation, but merely his own person. This is likely why Satan went immediately for those who were given dominion. Being an enemy of God (thus an enemy of those who bear His image), he apparently wanted to do the most damage, so it was likely that his deception happened quickly.

The responsibility of Adam

Adam failed at his responsibilities in two ways. He should have stopped his wife from eating, since he was there to observe exactly what she said and was about to eat (Genesis 3:6). Instead of listening to and correcting the words of his wife (Genesis 3:17), he ate without being deceived (1 Timothy 2:14).

Adam also arguably failed to keep/guard the garden as he was commanded in Genesis 2:15. God, knowing Satan would fall, gave this command to Adam, but Adam did not complete the task. But God even knew that Adam would fall short and had a plan specially prepared.

I've had some people ask me, "Why do we have to die for something Adam did?" The answer is simple—we are without excuse since we sin, too (Romans 3:23, 5:12). But then some have asked, "Why did we have to inherit sin nature from Adam, which is why we sin?" We read in Hebrews:

> Even Levi, who receives tithes, paid tithes through Abraham, so to speak, for he was still in the loins of his father when Melchizedek met him (Hebrews 7:9–10).

If we follow this logic, then all of us were ultimately in Adam when he sinned. So, although we often blame Adam, the life we have was in Adam when he sinned, and the sin nature we received was because we were in Adam when he sinned. We share in the blame and the sin as well as the punishment.

But look back further. The life that we (including Eve) have, came through Adam and ultimately came from God (Genesis 2:17). God owns us and gives us our very being (Hebrews 1:3), and it is He whom we should follow instead of our own sinful inclinations. Since this first sin, we have had the need for a Savior, Jesus Christ, the Son of God who would step into history to become a man and take the punishment for humanity's sin. Such a loving feat shows that God truly loves mankind and wants to see us return to Him. God—being the Author of life, the Sustainer of life, and Redeemer of life—is truly the Oneto whom we owe all things.

Were Satan and the Angels Created in the "Image of God"?

by Bodie Hodge

The image of God

Being made in the image of God is a major factor distinguishing humanity from the animals and other physical entities. In Genesis 1:26–27, we read:

> Then God said, "Let Us make man in Our image, according to Our likeness; let them have dominion over the fish of the sea, over the birds of the air, and over the cattle, over all the earth and over every creeping thing that creeps on the earth." So God created man in His own image; in the image of God He created him; male and female He created them.

According to verse 27, both Adam and the Woman (male and female) were created in the image of God. Since we are all descendants of our first parents, then we have been made in the image of God as well. Genesis 9:6 confirms that the image of God is passed on to Adam's descendants.

What sets us apart from animals and plants is that we have a spiritual aspect. Plants have a "body" or at least a physical aspect but no soul. This is why creationists often point out that plants are not living in the biblical sense. Animals, on the other hand, were created with a body and a soul (Hebrew: *nephesh*) according to such passages as Genesis 1:24–25. Unlike animals, humanity has a spiritual aspect as well.[1] Recall Paul's letter to the Thessalonians:

> May God himself, the God of peace, sanctify you through and through. May your whole spirit, soul, and body be kept blameless at the coming of our Lord Jesus Christ (1 Thessalonians 5:23).

Mankind has a unique, spiritual aspect, and this spirit is uniquely made in the image of God.[2] We should expect this image to have certain aspects of God's characteristics since God is spirit (John 4:24). However, this does not mean that we have all of them, for we have but a taste of God's attributes. This image was first placed into Adam when God breathed life into him.

> And the LORD God formed man of the dust of the ground, and breathed into his nostrils the breath (spirit) of life; and man became a living being (Genesis 2:7).

The Hebrew word for *breath* here is *nashamah* and is often translated as "breath" or "spirit." Often Christians describe the image of God as superior intellectual ability, such as reason and abstract thought, worship of God, language and communication with God, ability to make decisions, creative expression, immortality, emotions such as love, sadness, anger, and so on. These attributes show how separate man is from beasts and other physical entities; however, angels, Satan, demons, and other heavenly host, have many of these same attributes.

Spiritual beings . . . image of God, too?

One may quickly dismiss such an intriguing question without much thought by claiming that the Bible doesn't say angels were created in the "image of God." However, a quick dismissal may be unwise. After all, the Scriptures do not say they *weren't* created in the image of God either. The Bible doesn't give us extensive

---

background about angels since its focus is on mankind, but we can examine what it does tell us about angels in attempting to answer this question.

Consider a few of these characteristics and see how Scripture ascribes them to spiritual beings. While many examples can be found in Scripture, a couple should suffice for each.

Superior intellectual ability such as reason and abstract thought

When the serpent, which was influenced by Satan, deceived Eve in Genesis 3, there was considerable intellectual ability, even being termed "clever/cunning." Satan, referring to Job in Job 1:9–11 and Job 2:4–5, used logic to say that Job would turn if he lost his possessions and became diseased. (Many people in such a situation probably would have turned from God, but God knew Job would not.)

Worship of God

Hebrews 1:6 points out that angels worship the Lord. We also see the heavenly host praising God in Luke 2:13–14.

Language and communication with God

Satan was able to converse with God in Job 1–2. Satan was also able to understand Christ (Mark 8:33). The legion of demons spoke with Christ (Mark 5:9). Angels often spoke to people, e.g. Mary, the mother of Christ, and John in Revelation.

Ability to make decisions

Satan and the demons obviously fell from grace when sinning against God.

Creative expression

The four living creatures (who are among the heavenly host) in Revelation 5:8–10 played harps and sang a new song. With the extensive amount of praise and worship to God by the angels and heavenly host, we would expect them to create much music—even the morning stars (i.e. angels) sang for joy at the creation (Job 38:7).

Immortality

Like humans, eternal life will be the outcome of angels who did not fall and eternal punishment for Satan and his angels (Matthew 25:41; Revelation 20:10).

Emotions such as love, joy, desire, sadness, pride, and anger

Luke 15:10 indicates that angels are joyous when one person repents. The devil has great wrath in Revelation 12:12. The angels and the devil have desires (1 Peter 1:12; John 8:44).

Conclusion

Since the Bible doesn't say whether spiritual beings are made in the image of God, we can only infer from Scripture. Of the many attributes Christians often cite as distinctions between mankind and animals as evidence that man is made in the image of God, these same attributes are found in heavenly beings. Though God only said man was made in the image of God.

Put simply, in our fallen state, we may never fully grasp what encompasses being made "in the image of God." God is infinite, and simply trying to comprehend God's attributes can sometimes seem overwhelming.

But on the flip side, should it be a surprise that spiritual beings have attributes of their Creator who is spirit as well? We can be sure of what God's Word teaches: humans are made in the image of God and are distinct from animals by having a spiritual aspect. I'm not aware of any major theological problems if one considers spiritual beings as being made in the image of God. But I would say this with hesitation. Therefore, it may be wise to leave open the possibility that heavenly beings are made in the image of God but without being dogmatic by any means.

---

1. We are not taking an official position on whether man is dichotomous (body and soul/spirit; where soul and spirit are merely interchangeable words of the same substance) or trichotomous (body, soul, and spirit; where each are truly separate and unique). This is a disputed issue among theologians and there doesn't seem to be a clear answer to it. Personally, I would lean toward a view that incorporates both in a unique way. The spirit would be a modified aspect of the soul, like a flip side of the same coin. There is one coin but two unique sides to it. In other words, our soul is specially fashioned with a spiritual aspect, like duality. So soul and spirit could almost be used interchangeably (being two parts to the same "coin"), which we find in Scripture (Luke 1:36–47). Yet soul and spirit could be seen as unique (two sides of the "coin"), which we also find in Scripture (1 Thessalonians 5:23; Hebrews 4:12). Of course, a thorough treatment of this subject would require much more than this short footnote.

2. In some cases in Scripture, spirit and soul are used almost interchangeably, but not always. This seems to indicate that the spiritual aspect may be a modified part of the soul, such as the flip side of a coin; this is why human souls with a spiritual aspect (made in the image of God) are truly unique to the souls of animals (merely *nephesh chayyah*). Although this subject deserves a paper in its own right, it is not for the discussion here.

Did the Serpent Tempt Eve While in the Tree?

by Bodie Hodge

Christians generally use illustrations of the Garden of Eden that place the serpent in a tree—usually the tree of the knowledge of good and evil. In fact, we do so at the Creation Museum in Petersburg, Kentucky.

Is there any justification for such a view?

What does Scripture say?

Nowhere in the Scriptures do we read that the serpent was in the tree—any tree. In fact, the opposite may well be deduced, as the serpent was compared to the beasts of the field twice:

> Now the serpent was more cunning than any beast *of the field* which the LORD God had made. And he said to the woman, "Has God indeed said, 'You shall not eat of every tree of the garden'?" (Genesis 3:1; emphasis mine).

> So the LORD God said to the serpent: "Because you have done this, you are cursed more than all cattle, and more than *every beast of the field*; On your belly you shall go, and you shall eat dust all the days of your life" (Genesis 3:14; emphasis mine).

If the Bible compares the serpent with beasts of the field, then it may well have been one. For the most part, beasts of the field are simply that: beasts found in the field. However, we must leave open the possibility that some of the beasts of the field could have climbed trees. After all, we cannot be sure of all the animals that fall into this category. So, this alone doesn't necessarily rule out the serpent being in the tree when it deceived Eve.

If we look closer at the initial stages of the deception by the serpent, we find:

> Now the serpent was more cunning than any beast of the field which the LORD God had made. And he said to the woman, "Has God indeed said, 'You shall not eat of every tree of the garden'?" And the woman said to the serpent, "We may eat the fruit of the trees of the garden; but of the fruit of the tree which is in the midst of the garden, God has said, 'You shall not eat it, nor shall you touch it, lest you die'" (Genesis 3:1–3).

Pay close attention to what Eve said here. She refers to the tree in the *midst* of the garden. Why would she say it like this if she were referring to a tree that the serpent is sitting in? If the serpent were really in the tree, then it makes more sense that she would respond something like: "We may eat the fruit of the trees of the garden; but of the fruit of the tree *which you are sitting in*, God has said, 'You shall not eat it, nor shall you touch it, lest you die.'"

Of course, the Scriptures do not reveal the exact location of their discussion, but instead point to a tree elsewhere *in the midst* of the Garden—perhaps not too far off.

Now, this may be a strong argument against the serpent being in the tree; however, we still cannot completely rule out the possibility. If some insist that the serpent had to be in the tree, then they can certainly put forward an argument. On the other hand, most images of the serpent tempting Eve from the tree are likely for dramatic impact. It's just good to keep what Scripture teaches in mind.

What Was the First Sin?

by Troy Lacey

Often when Christians think of the first sin, they think of Adam and Eve and the Fall in the Garden of Eden. While this is indeed the first human sin, it is not the first recorded sin in Scripture. As Christians, we know that the serpent tempted Eve, but we often forget that the devil's fall from grace was what set the stage for humankind's fall, both as antecedent and type.

We catch a glimpse of Satan's fall in the following passage, prophetically directed at the king of Tyre. But this portion was apparently meant to include a non-human (specifically referred to as a *cherub*) who had been in the Garden of Eden. The prophecy turns into a description of an angel, namely Lucifer:

> You were the anointed cherub who covers; I established you; you were on the holy mountain of God; you walked back and forth in the midst of fiery stones. You were perfect in your ways from the day you were created, till iniquity was found in you (Ezekiel 28:14–15).

What was the first sin? We learn about it and Satan's fall from Isaiah 14:12–15:

> How you are fallen from heaven, O Lucifer, son of the morning! How you are cut down to the ground, you who weakened the nations! For you have said in your heart: "I will ascend into heaven, I will exalt my throne above the stars of God; I will also sit on the mount of the congregation on the farthest sides of the north; I will ascend above the heights of the clouds, I will be like the Most High." Yet you shall be brought down to Sheol, to the lowest depths of the Pit.

It is obvious from the text that Satan's sin was pride. He was so beautiful, so wise, and so powerful as an angel that he began to covet God's position and authority. He chafed at having to serve God and grew angry and rebellious. He did not want to serve, he wanted to be served; he, as a creature, wanted to be worshipped. How starkly contrasted to our Savior, Jesus Christ, who came not to be served, but to serve and to give his life a ransom for many (Mark 10:45).

How did Satan's prideful rebellion and subsequent fall impact humankind's first sin? Look at some passages in Proverbs that talk about the sin of pride and what effect it produces:

Proverbs 16:18—Pride goes before destruction, and a haughty spirit before a fall.

Proverbs 11:2—When pride comes, then comes shame: but with the humble is wisdom.

Proverbs 18:12—Before destruction the heart of man is haughty, and before honor is humility.

Here, it is evident that pride literally went before the Fall, both the fall of Satan and the fall of man. Pride causes shame, loss of wisdom, destruction, and ruin. If we were to summarize what actually happened as Adam and Eve were kicked out of the Garden of Eden, wouldn't these passages describe their mental and physical condition exactly? Shamed by the knowledge of committing sin against God, physical disease, pain, and death looming on the horizon, loss of fellowship with God, and having to fight to eke out a living from the cursed ground; all these are the outworkings of the sin of pride.

So, what was Adam and Eve's sin? Wasn't it just disobedience by eating the forbidden fruit? Well, yes, that was the physical act that solidified what had already occurred in their minds and hearts. But let's take a closer look at the passages in Genesis to see what the real sin was and where it started:

¹ Now the serpent was more cunning than any beast of the field which the Lord God had made. And he said to the woman, "Has God indeed said, 'You shall not eat of every tree of the garden'?" ² And the woman said to the serpent, "We may eat the fruit of the trees of the garden; ³ but of the fruit of the tree which is in the midst of the garden, God has said, 'You shall not eat it, nor shall you touch it, lest you die.'" ⁴ Then the serpent said to the woman, "You will not surely die. ⁵ For God knows that in the day you eat of it your eyes will be opened, and you will be like God, knowing good and evil." ⁶ So when the woman saw that the tree was good for food, that it was pleasant to the eyes, and a tree desirable to make one wise, she took of its fruit and ate. She also gave to her husband with her, and he ate. ⁷ Then the eyes of both of them were opened, and they knew that they were naked; and they sewed fig leaves together and made themselves coverings. . . . ¹² Then the man said, "The woman whom You gave to be with me, she gave me of the tree, and I ate." ¹³ And the Lord God said to the woman, "What is this you have done?" The woman said, "The serpent deceived me, and I ate" (Genesis 3:1–7, 3:12–13).

Let's analyze what really happened in verses 1–7. First Satan questioned God's Word, then he openly lied to Eve, contradicting what God had said. Then he used the tantalizing bait that humanity could be more like God by having their eyes opened, knowing things they currently didn't know. The real heart of the situation is the statement that Eve thought the tree was good for food and desirable to make one wise. Why would she think this? God himself had told Adam (and either God himself or Adam had told Eve), that eating from the tree would only lead to death. Why would she (and subsequently Adam) accept the word of a talking serpent over the Word of God? Only doubt of God's Word and God's motives could have led to this tragedy.

They didn't just ignorantly decide to eat the fruit, nor did they eat it because "the devil made them do it." Satan's outright lies and cunning half-truths brought something to the surface of Eve's mind that fateful day. She realized that to "be like gods" meant not having to serve God, it meant being equal to God. It meant that she felt as if God had deliberately kept her and Adam in the dark regarding their "divine potential." Why should they tend God's garden in Eden when they could be as gods themselves? Why should they have to obey God if they were also gods? The quickness with which Adam acquiesced to Eve's offer of the fruit may possibly show that he, too, harbored these same feelings, or it may mean that Adam, though knowing Eve had sinned willfully decided to throw his lot in with her by deliberately eating from the fruit. Eve had been deceived, Adam had not. In any event, we know that it was Adam's sin that was responsible for the Fall and the Curse (Romans 5:12). The sin of pride that led to Satan's fall had now infected the hearts and minds of Adam and Eve, and the result was the same: shame, loss of wisdom, ruin, and death.

In verses 12 and 13, we see Adam and Eve's response to God's question. We see the sin of pride showing through in their replies. This isn't just a pass-the-buck response on their part; look at whom they really blamed for their actions: "The serpent deceived me," said Eve. "The woman *you* gave to be with me enticed me," said Adam. They almost seem to say that if they had been God, things would have been different; therefore, it's all God's fault. These are not the responses of broken and contrite hearts, they are the responses of proud and willful people caught in the act of rebellion against God.

What is still man's most prevalent sin? Little has changed since the Fall. Man is still a creature consumed with pride. We read in Romans 1:18–21 the current condition of mankind:

> For the wrath of God is revealed from heaven against all
> ungodliness and unrighteousness of men, who suppress the

truth in unrighteousness, because what may be known of God is manifest in them, for God has shown it to them. For since the creation of the world His invisible attributes are clearly seen, being understood by the things that are made, even His eternal power and Godhead, so that they are without excuse, because, although they knew God, they did not glorify Him as God, nor were thankful, but became futile in their thoughts, and their foolish hearts were darkened.

Why does mankind suppress the truth? Why does he not glorify God? Why is he unthankful? Why is his imagination vain and his heart darkened? Because he does not glorify God as God. Mankind wants to glorify himself as God. We want to be the sole decision maker and sole authority in our life. We want nothing to do with a Creator God to whom we should owe allegiance. If only we could come up with some natural explanation for everything we see around us; if only we could ignore our conscience; if only we could forget past history that clearly shows divine intervention; then we could rationalize away God and make gods of ourselves. Isn't this exactly what we see today? Now we have evolution, moral relativism, humanism, revisionist history, and all other attempts to willfully hold God's revealed truth at arm's length. Truly our sinful human pride knows no bounds!

The Lord knows where his creatures are most prone to err, and pride is a many-headed hydra that infects all of humanity. In fact, we could make a case for pride being the fountainhead of all other sins. Anger, hate, jealousy, and ingratitude all stem from pride; something we wanted to happen did not happen, and we feel offended; our pride is wounded and our emotions are stirred to cause us to act sinfully. One could even make the case that "the love of money is the root of all [kinds of] evil" passage in 1 Timothy 6:10 really deals with the sin of pride as well. We know that covetousness is the same as idolatry (Ephesians 5:5), and idolatry is the sin of creating our own god by being too proud and stubborn to worship the True God. Consider the following verses in Proverbs that reflect God's attitude toward pride.

> These six things the Lord hates, yes, seven are an abomination to Him: a proud look, a lying tongue, hands that shed innocent blood, a heart that devises wicked plans, feet that are swift in running to evil, a false witness who speaks lies, and one who sows discord among brethren (Proverbs 6:16–19).

> The fear of the Lord is to hate evil; pride and arrogance and the evil way and the perverse mouth I hate (Proverbs 8:13).

On God's top seven list of most heinous sins, pride comes in at number one! In verse 13 we see that the fear of the Lord is equated with hating pride and arrogance. If we allow pride to control us, we do not really fear God as we ought. C. S. Lewis said,

> The essential vice, the utmost evil, is Pride. Unchastity, greed, drunkenness, and all that, are mere flea-bites in comparison: it was through Pride that the devil became the devil: Pride leads to every other vice: it is the complete anti-God state of mind.

What should we as Christians do to guard against this sin? There are no instant cures for this sin. Pride is a sin we struggle with on a daily basis. (Read Romans 7:13–25 to see how the Apostle Paul agonizes over his struggles against sin, and also think of the "thorn in the flesh" in 2 Corinthians 12:7 that was given to Paul to keep him from becoming exalted above measure.) However, God doesn't leave us or forsake us. He gives us grace and power to overcome even this most insidious sin. A couple of passages in James and 1 Peter deal with this very subject:

> Or do you think that the Scripture says in vain, "The Spirit who dwells in us yearns jealously"? But He gives more grace. Therefore He says: "God resists the proud, but gives grace to the humble." Therefore submit to God. Resist the

devil and he will flee from you. Draw near to God and He will draw near to you. Cleanse your hands, you sinners; and purify your hearts, you double-minded (James 4:5–8).

Likewise you younger people, submit yourselves to your elders. Yes, all of you be submissive to one another, and be clothed with humility, for "God resists the proud, but gives grace to the humble." Therefore humble yourselves under the mighty hand of God, that He may exalt you in due time, casting all your care upon Him, for He cares for you. Be sober, be vigilant; because your adversary the devil walks about like a roaring lion, seeking whom he may devour. Resist him, steadfast in the faith, knowing that the same sufferings are experienced by your brotherhood in the world. But may the God of all grace, who called us to His eternal glory by Christ Jesus, after you have suffered a while, perfect, establish, strengthen, and settle you (1 Peter 5:5–10).

It is only through God's grace and provision that we can daily overcome our innate pride. We need to pray (cast all our cares upon God), study the Bible (be sober and vigilant), be submissive to God by obeying Him and revering Him, and recognize that it is Jesus Christ who strengthens, establishes, settles, and perfects us. Without Him we can do nothing!

It is interesting that in both of the above passages we are warned to forsake pride and humbly submit ourselves before God in order to resist the devil. Why this twofold warning? We give Satan a foothold when we walk more like him than like Christ (who came to do not His own will but the will of the Father). Secondly, playing to human pride is the oldest trick in Satan's arsenal. Just ask Adam and Eve.

Do Verses in Ezekiel and Isaiah Refer to Earthly Kings or Satan?

by Troy Lacey

The first thing that needs to be addressed is the nature of biblical prophecies. Unlike historical narrative (such as Genesis), they often contain much figurative language. But also, many prophecies do have a near and far fulfillment. Take, for example, Psalm 22 describing not only David's own troubles with his enemies and how he felt about it, but also describing Christ's death on the Cross over 1,000 years later.

In studying Ezekiel 28 and Isaiah 14 for "The First Sin," numerous commentaries and Bible margin notes were consulted, as well as checking for context in the passages themselves. The vast majority of these reference tools concur that in both of these passages, Satan is the ultimate focus in these prophecies, though, of course, the scholars all readily see that the king of Tyre and the king of Babylon, respectively, are in view also (at least with part of the prophecies). Conservative scholarship through the ages has by and large attributed these passages to statements concerning past actions and past or future judgment against Satan.

The Ezekiel passage is a lament regarding the king of Tyrus (Tyre), most probably Ittobaal II, but the prophecy extends far beyond the immediate king and includes attributes that could not and do not apply to a mortal man. For example, in Ezekiel 28:13, it is stated that this being was in "Eden the Garden of God;" according to the scriptural record only God, Adam, Eve,

Satan, and the two Cherubim placed there to guard it were ever in Eden. Ittobaal II certainly was not.

Also, in verse 14, this being is referred to as a cherub; no man is ever referred to as a cherub anywhere else in Scripture. With the possible exception of the "angels" of the churches in Revelation 2–3, no man is ever clearly called an angel (scholars seem to be divided on whether these are the elders of the churches or actual guardian angels). Even if this were the case, it may not be wise to argue semantics of a Greek word in application to a Hebrew word used in Ezekiel.

In verse 15, the being is described as perfect in all his ways—until iniquity was found in him. This means that this being was created (not born) perfect, and remained so until he sinned. This statement could only apply to Adam, Eve, Satan, or demons, not to any earthly king. The king of Tyre was "shaped in iniquity and conceived in sin," just like all other humans (Psalm 51:5). While it probably is true that the king of Tyre was the immediate target of the prophecy (at least in part), and while it may be possible that he exhibited many characteristics of Satan (pride and deceitfulness), the ultimate "woe" of this lament is directed at Satan—and this is not unprecedented. Jesus spoke directly to Legion (Mark 5:1–14) and directly to Satan when he was influencing Peter (Mark 8:33). Also, Daniel 10:13 indicates demonic forces are behind (at least some) political leaders and Ephesians 6:11–12 strongly suggests the same. So, the idea that Satan was working behind and through the king of Tyre and that the prophecy was about both is not a ridiculous notion.

The passage in Isaiah 14 is a proverb or taunt addressed to the king of Babylon (verse 4). But, again, the prophecy goes beyond the description of a mortal man. Verse 12 states that Lucifer ("the shining one" or "the day star") had fallen from heaven. Mortal men do not fall from heaven; however, twice we read of Satan falling from (or being thrown out of) heaven (Luke 10:18; Revelation

12:9). It is highly unlikely that a mortal man could honestly think that he could ascend into heaven and dethrone God, as this Lucifer thought, according to verses 13 and 14. Ultimately, the creature that is being addressed here is Satan, the shining one, who disguises himself as an angel of light (2 Corinthians 11:14). Regardless of the play on words, Lucifer can rightly be used as a name as well. Most of God's names that He reveals constitute a play on words as well (e.g., *Jehovah Jireh* means the Lord provides, etc.).

I do understand that there is not 100% agreement on these passages, but the majority of Christian scholarship down through the ages has either actively promoted or accepted this understanding of these two prophecies. There was, however, one concordance reviewed (Jamiesson, Faucett, and Brown) that did not hold the position that these passages speak about Satan. Instead, they hold the position that the prophecies were ultimately directed at the Antichrist, while being immediately directed at the kings of Tyre and Babylon. So, they still see a near and far fulfillment.

To us there seems to be both strong biblical reasons and confirmation from the history of Christian interpretation that Satan was the one influencing these kings and is the ultimate subject of these prophecies.

Troy Lacey works in the Correspondence department at Answers in Genesis and writes occasional article for the AiG website. He holds a BS in Natural Sciences (Geology and Microbiology) from the University of Cincinnati.

Did the Serpent in the Garden Have Anything to Do with Satan?

by Troy Lacey

The book of Genesis does not mention the name or title "Satan," nor does it specifically state that Lucifer or any demonic being controlled the serpent in the Garden of Eden. Having said that, however, we can ascertain who this serpent was (or rather who was controlling and speaking through this serpent) from other passages of Scripture, and from the context of Genesis 3 itself.

Ezekiel 28:13 states that the being addressed was listed as being in Eden, the Garden of God. If this passage is talking about Satan, then there is a clear reference to Satan being in the Garden of Eden. Since Satan was a created being, and since Eden was guarded by cherubim after the Fall, he must have been in Eden between his creation and the Fall of man. Many scholars believe, based on Job 38:7, that all the angels, including Lucifer, were created on or before Day 3 of Creation Week prior to the sun, moon and stars, only at least three days before the creation of Adam and Eve.

Secondly, Satan is called a serpent, not once but three times in the book of Revelation (Revelation 12:9, 12:15, 20:2). When combined with Paul's words in 2 Corinthians 11:3, the identification of the serpent in Genesis 3 with Satan is unmistakable.

> So the great dragon was cast out, that serpent of old, called the devil and Satan, who deceives the whole world; he was cast to the earth, and his angels were cast out with him (Revelation 12:9.

But I fear, lest somehow, as the serpent deceived Eve by his craftiness, so your minds may be corrupted from the simplicity that is in Christ (2 Corinthians 11:3).

We see an obvious parallel here with Genesis 3. Revelation 12:9 says that Satan is called "that serpent of old," that he was punished (cast out), and that he presently deceives the whole world (remember that Adam and Eve were even the "whole world" of humanity at the time of the Fall). Revelation 20:2–3 also calls Satan a serpent and speaks of his punishment again. This time he will be bound and thrown into the bottomless pit for 1,000 years so that he will not be able to deceive the nations. Satan's work of deception began in the Garden of Eden and has continued worldwide ever since then. Only Christians can escape Satan's deceptions by simple and pure devotion to Christ (i.e., trusting and obeying His Word by His Spirit).

Finally, in Genesis 3:14–15 we read of God's curse upon the serpent and the promise of a Savior from the seed of the woman.

So the LORD God said to the serpent: "Because you have done this, you are cursed more than all cattle, and more than every beast of the field; on your belly you shall go, and you shall eat dust all the days of your life. And I will put enmity between you and the woman, and between your seed and her Seed; He shall bruise your head, and you shall bruise His heel" (Genesis 3:14–15).

The prediction of enmity (hatred and warfare) between the seeds (in some sense offspring or descendant) of the woman and of the serpent makes no sense if the serpent were merely a physical animal. The seed of the woman is a future male child. If only serpents and natural human descendants are in view here, then that means that snakes are doomed to go around biting men in the heels and then getting their heads crushed. Given the verses in Revelation and 2 Corinthians, this obviously is not the intent of the prophecy.

Christian orthodoxy has always understood this to be the first prophecy of the Messiah, who would be the Savior of the world. Satan did bruise Jesus on the heel (so to speak), by moving men to crucify Him. But it was only a temporary wound, for He rose from the dead. But the same act by which Satan thought he had defeated Jesus Christ, was the very act by which Jesus destroyed the power of Satan, and His Resurrection was the proof and seal of that victory. One day the full results of that victory will be realized when Satan's head will be crushed in the sense that he will be cast into the lake of fire where he will be tormented day and night, forever (Revelation 20:10).

Were All Snakes Condemned to Crawl on Their Belly?

by Troy Lacey

Creationists do not say that the original created kinds have not changed since Creation. It is clear from Scripture and from the study of living things that God implanted a great capacity for change and adaptation in the DNA of created kinds.

We see this, for example, in the great variety within the cat and dog kinds or the variety within mankind. There is great variation within each kind, but one kind does not change into a different kind. Cats reproduce cats, dogs reproduce dogs, and people reproduce people.

But Genesis 3 also makes it clear that because of God's curse on all of creation, the serpent was physically changed (to crawl on his belly), the woman was changed physically (increased pain in childbirth), and both man and woman were changed physically so that their bodies began the process of decay leading to eventual death. Given that God also cursed the other animals (Genesis 3:14), they undoubtedly were changed physically in some ways also, e.g., some herbivores became carnivores sometime after the Fall.

Genesis 3 teaches us about Satan's deception of Eve, the sin of Adam, God's judgment of the whole creation, and His first promise of the coming Messiah to overcome the work of Satan and the sin inherited from Adam that infects us all. That freedom comes to us when we turn from our sin and put our trust in Jesus Christ as our Savior and Lord.

HOLY
BIBLE

What Is the Good News?

Answers in Genesis seeks to give glory and honor to God as Creator, and to affirm the truth of the biblical record of the real origin and history of the world and mankind.

Part of this real history is the bad news that the rebellion of the first man, Adam, against God's command brought death, suffering, and separation from God into this world. We see the results all around us. All of Adam's descendants are sinful from conception (Psalm 51:5) and have themselves entered into this rebellion (sin). They, therefore, cannot live with a holy God but are condemned to separation from God. The Bible says that "all have sinned, and come short of the glory of God" (Romans 3:23) and that all are therefore subject to "everlasting destruction from the presence of the Lord and from the glory of His power" (2 Thessalonians 1:9).

But the good news is that God has done something about it.

> For God so loved the world, that He gave his only-begotten Son, that whoever believes in Him should not perish, but have everlasting life (John 3:16).

Jesus Christ the Creator, though totally sinless, suffered, on behalf of mankind, the penalty of mankind's sin, which is death and separation from God. He did this to satisfy the righteous demands of the holiness and justice of God, His Father. Jesus was the perfect sacrifice; He died on a cross, but on the third day, He rose again, conquering death so that all who truly believe in Him, repent of their sin, and trust in Him (rather than their own merit) are able to come back to God and live for eternity with their Creator.

Therefore:

> He who believes on Him is not condemned, but he who does not believe is condemned already, because he has not believed in the name of the only-begotten Son of God (John 3:18).

What a wonderful Savior—and what a wonderful salvation in Christ, our Creator!

If you want to know more of what the Bible says about how *you* can receive eternal life, please write or call Answers in Genesis.